UN-SILENCED

POEMS

ELIZABETH LUND

Červená Barva Press

Somerville, Massachusetts

Červená Barva Press
P.O. Box 440357
W. Somerville, MA 02144-3222

www.cervenabarvapress.com

Bookstore: www.thelostbookshelf.com

Cover Art: "Interior with Ida in a White Chair" by Vilhelm Hammershøi (1900)

Cover Design: William J. Kelle

ISBN: 978-1-950063-79-6

Library of Congress Control Number: 2022942674

"When people don't express themselves, they die one piece at a time."

— Laurie Halse Anderson

Acknowledgments

Poems in this collection have appeared or are forthcoming in the following publications:

The Christian Century: "Underwater"

The Christian Science Monitor: "Berries" (an earlier version)

Connecticut Review: "Reaching"

The Dalhousie Review: "Your eyes shall be opened"

Kalliope: "Strays"

Painted Hills Review: "Homecoming" (an earlier version)

Paterson Literary Review: "Interrogation"

Salamander: "In the dream he's a blacksmith"

SpoKe: "After one year"; "At the animal park, Rte. 13"; "Auntie"; "Driving to Winnipesaukee"; "40th anniversary"; "Refrain"; "Remembering Elaine"; "Steam"; "The fittest"; "This will cost you"; "Two owls in conversation"; "Woman in the center of the orchid"

Thank you to the editors who first published some of the poems in this collection.

Many thanks to Gloria Mindock, editor and publisher, and everyone at Červená Barva Press, for their support of my work.

I'm deeply grateful for several friends and fellow poets who provided helpful comments as this manuscript evolved, especially Hilary Holladay, who read an early draft, and Bg Thurston, who helped me throughout the process and with the finishing work.

Finally, my unending appreciation for my dear friend Pat and my husband, Chris, for their unwavering love and encouragement.

Table of Contents

A Chorus Rising

The Niece Finds Her Voice

UN-SILENCED

Remembering Elaine

One great blue heron
punctuates the shore,
huddling in first snow.

What keeps this steel-eyed
juvenile here, weeks after
the others have flown?

Gray on gray she stands
like a wrought-iron
question mark.

What does she read
in the tinfoil sky,
its indecipherable script?

Does she stand, like me,
awaiting a sign, has she
hunkered too far down?

How do winged creatures
lose their lift, their bold
exclamation point?

One could say the sky
turns a deaf ear, that some
stories are meant to trail off.

She stands ramrod straight,
like a stubborn suicide
or a righteous sacrifice.

But I'm not ready to let
her go, as the season's
first storm spits and swirls.

THE SECRETS SHE KEPT

Breaking news

No one knew the word *lockdown*
then, how fear traps you inside.

One station blared, "Neighbors shocked,"
while two copters buzzed above.

One paper wrote, "Red flags missed."
Another said, "Wife's parting shot."

For three days, the only fact
they got right: Elaine was 69.

Every time they killed her again
I pictured her weeks earlier, stirring

in the kitchen. A barred owl outside
the window says, *I love hearing you*

laugh, ma'am, so mischievous, unafraid.
Can that woman stay when he returns?

Details at 5, 6, 11.

Homecoming

The day he returned, limping over
the threshold, there was no hint,

no horizon. Just wind and sleet slashing
at winter trees. Disapproval, caution?

I need to climb this staircase again,
he said as she stared out the window.

Umbrellas bloomed on the pavement.
Red, navy, black. Inverted boats.

As if they knew some illnesses lie
dormant, plotting for years in silence.

Assassins

Those people on the TV told him,
Two shots will stop your pain.

No side effects, so easy.
His hundreds of metal soldiers agreed.

We guarded the house when you were
in rehab. Just as you trained us to do.

One by one he inspected his men,
uniforms starched, weapons drawn.

When will your hip work again, sir?
We're ready to fight when you are.

Day after day he reddened their lips,
blackened eyes, straightened their guns.

Soon, boys. Hold your position.
Enemy in the kitchen.

Premonition

Days before he dialed 9-1-1,
she thrashed and gasped in dreams.

Each night she'd reach as if riding a wave,
then tumble headfirst on the sand.

Tsunami coming, a distant voice said.
Nothing will help you then.

9-1-1, what is your emergency?

Somebody needs to take care of him.
I can't do it on my own.

The fittest

"Animals respond to a gentle voice,"
she'd say as one shook on her lap.

Figaro, Daisy, Magic.
She coaxed and captured them all.

Princess, Blackie, Snowball.
Saved from the side of the road.

One tiger followed her everywhere,
a shadow leaving the room.

Another hid under the sofa
until she was all alone.

"Love them until they can rule
the savannah. Always a gentle voice."

Elaine, lost Queen of the jungle,
you should have roared, or run.

Steam

Began with one tiny bubble
breaking the fragile calm.

Another bead, another deep breath
till pock marks danced in the pan.

Help me feed our child, she said.
Third-degree burn on her wrist.

Steam swirled like a funnel cloud.
Lion's head shook and roared.

Help me change the bandage, she pleaded
as bottles boiled on the stove.

Another wound, another short breath.
Skin bloody as a gazelle's neck.

Why won't you help me?
Her blisters wept.

The answer stung for years.

Auxiliary

He always hated that damn word
on his 8-point hat and badge.

A-U-X—who did this to him?
Crucifix turned sideways.

Don't you know who I am?
Denied every year. D-E-N-I-E-D.

Was it wisdom or premonition
that made the police chief say,

"He can do traffic. No gun, ever.
He's too short-fused to carry."

That Sunday

Five of us bounce, bounced in the car
while he lowered himself down, down.

To the lake, he said, tossing a kiss
while honk, honking the horn.

She looked like a sunflower,
face turned toward the warmth.

Periwinkle sky swallowed us all
as we rolled, rolled out the yard.

For years she held, held that moment.
Her perfect husband. Once.

Berries

That day she was given the river,
the brush. Picked the fullest orbs,
named them Joy, Laughter.

What did she owe for solitary
pleasures? Palms stained,
knees blood-webbed.

40th anniversary

Sky was the color of worn silver that day
a barn owl tangled with barbed wire.

He screeched and flapped at his white-
faced mate until red flowed from wing to feet.

Take her instead of me.
Break this thorny cage.

Years of begging, bargaining,
a flight too long and low.

Make him be good to me.
Or fly far, far away.

Clouds roll past, face down.
Tails, you lose. Heads, he wins.

Such is the cost of gambling:
Yet you roll the dice again.

Her one complaint

No one ever told me
I'd married Beelzebub.

Never warned, "serpent's tongue
starts to sound like yourself."

Stupid, worthless wench, he says.
Lucky that I love you.

Deception coils slowly.
Fork-tongued tempter. Liar.

He stops talking, I chime in:
"Stupid, worthless woman."

Ye shall not eat of it . . .

At night she was a second Eve.
Sorrow swirling in her cup,
murky brown, deep enough
to drown in.

She'd slice a red apple
and halve it again.
He lay upstairs, snoring.

Seeds on the table
tucked under her knife,
each filled with
bitter temptation:

You chose poorly.
Too late now.
The penalty can't be lifted.

Warning

Silence is like a horror movie,
owl said from the top of the stairs.

Don't stand by the front door alone.
Don't let him take aim.

Sometimes we must flee without
maps, just one terrifying leap.

Sweeten up, she scolded him.
Heard the slide snap back.

Auntie

When police arrived, she hovered
just beneath the ceiling,
her *oh* and *no* struggling to rise.

I don't believe she taunted him,
waving an apron as if at a bull:
"Old man, you can't even shoot straight."

Forty-six years they had teetered
at the edge of a precipice.

Did silence scream, one last time,
nagging the spouse neither
wanted nor loved?

Or did she slump as he wavered:
his *oh* so soft and hideous
that only their tabby,
in the rafters, had any
chance to survive.

Refrain

the family removed all of his guns
thought they'd removed
all his guns

all the weapons
removed
they thought

all weapons
the family
removed

all but one
the newspaper said
all but

one

Where Gummy go?

the three-year-old asked.
Gummy? Where she go?

He thinks she stands
on the edge of a cloud,
poised to dive back down.

How do you say,
Never coming back . . .

weeks after he raised
clenched fists, shouting,
Leave my Gummy alone!

Sometimes, she was too tired
to pray: *Help me, I'm afraid.*

Other thoughts rose;
she pulled each one down
like a balloon on a string.

Just go. You can leave.
Please pick up the phone.

Arraignment

He shuffled slowly from the van,
hand reaching for a wall.

Please take these chains off me.
I'm just a frail old man.

He stumbled past a reporter.
I'd never hurt anyone.

A shock of blue in the courtroom.
Like a jay, he began to squawk.

What don't you people understand?
She threatened to stop cooking.

Proverbs 31 woman

After the yellow tape came down,
the back door slowly moaned.
Flashlight, cat food, cat carrier.
She had taught my cousins well.

"You can come out now," they cooed
in the kitchen where he'd reported murder-
suicide then gave himself a flesh wound.

"No one will hurt you," they said
in the pantry, freshly painted walnut
and turquoise, then down the cellar stairs.

In the parlor they called, "You're safe,"
peering behind his lemon-colored
armchair and under the aqua sofa
she had saved for years to buy.

Three toy soldiers lay there still,
guns pointed at the front door.
"We won't leave you here alone."
Her silhouette staining the floor.

He dreamed he was walking

through swarms of white locusts:
trees, houses, roads eaten.

Where did you hide my car?
he yelled, fumbling with
keys, accusations.

Open this goddam door.
Why are you still sleeping?

Hands pincer stiff, he clawed
at the lock. His cell
was a pot, simmering.

Pharaoh's seventh plague
raged on. *I will never let you go.*

The only sound, a plow
in the distance, yellow
arthropod crawling along.

Plea bargain

August heat in September.
Uncle David shackled in court.

*"Your honor, he's sorry for what
he's done. His children deserved better."*

What the defender didn't say is that
illnesses, like excuses, mutate to survive.

David moved one angry foot clockwise,
counter. Wrote *i-n-n-o-c-e-n-t* on the table.

He didn't blink when one daughter cried,
"She should be here, not you."

He traced *i-n-n* again when the other sister
said, *"You've brought this on yourself."*

The judge paused, narrowed his eyes.
Fifteen years. God have mercy on your soul.

Unanswered

Three days after he died in prison
her voice began to call.

Tell others not to make my mistake,
waiting silently for the slaughter.

A CHORUS RISING

Interrogation

For three weeks in March a barred owl kept watch
from a beech tree inside the barbed-wire fence.

Who comes for you? it asked every night
of the women trapped in their prison blues.

The question echoed across the empty yard:
Who comes for you or you or you?

Perhaps the bird divined lonely passings or knew
how lovers, friends, and children rarely visit.

Who comes for you or remembers your name?
the owl repeated until every brown leaf, still

clinging from last season, shriveled and fell
from the tree like an unspoken confession.

This will cost you

Change, change, it's all
about change, says the bard
from his Common bench.

Change, change, I bet you
want change, he demands
of a sunburned vet.

Who's that staggering
home, he asks of a financier
wearing scuffed wingtips.

A siege of girls in thin
pink heels, white pants
preens like hungry egrets.

Change, change, it's all
about change, he sings
again, jostling the blues.

A wispy blonde, one
arm in a sling, opens
her tiny red mouth.

Change, change. I like
that tune. But how
much will it cost?

Sonia's ballad

Sang his anger, sang his love.
Heart was hot, veins cold.

Baby, come here. Go away.
Always hot, then cold.

Icicles wept in February.
Days he wouldn't come home.

Hid her anger, sang her love.
Hate to be alone.

Baby, I need more than you.
Blizzard without snow.

No other man will want you.
Fear grew hot, heart cold.

Johnnie Walker

Call it the good-girl addiction:
Loved to rescue my man.

Each time he walked across
train tracks, warmth rose up

slid down. The burn
became sweeter, deeper

when he turned toward
the train's two bright eyes.

Come and get me, you mother.
How the danger intoxified.

Maria's mirage

No one understands why I stay.
He just needs a little more love.

Red bites, yellow bruises.
Blue lights slicing the sky.

He was never treated right.
Mother, father, friends.

Purple eyelids, scarlet scars.
Is that blood on the door?

Pay no mind. I tripped and fell.
He just needs a little more love.

Other women shift in their seats.
Sister, why can't you open your eyes?

Skins

He chooses another
apple to peel, saying
this one looks like
a woman's head.

He cuts away two
soft spots on top,
slices off a bump where
a nose might be, removes
extra flesh all around.

It can be this simple,
he insists, lifting a green
and red globe.

All it takes is practice
to remake every curve,
each uneven surface.

He begins at the top,
guiding the knife
till an unblemished
body appears in his hand.

Fruit by fruit, a new Eden
emerges. He is God
and flawless Adam.

He peels a new face for
one silent Eve, gives another
breasts firm and smooth.

Now that *is perfection,*
he says, waving the knife,
as if any woman could be
so easily reshaped.

Woman in the center of the orchid

Five dead sisters
surround her, their feet
tightly bound, lilac skin
bruised at every turn.

Like them, she's a virgin
trapped in a room
of rippled light and blood.

Her yellow head, hung
in prayer; hands open
on a purple-petal pulpit.

Every morning she bows
to the ground, prostrate
for matchmakers, future grooms.

At night she genuflects
again, skin tearing
as they tie her down.

Reaching

—Forest Hills Cemetery

When fog pulls its noose round the dead
and the buried, even God's jealous hand
can't save them, drawn as they are

to these winged women, stone-faced sirens
pushed out Gabriel's trapdoor.

Mapless pilgrims, they don't know better,
sailing after flawless faces as wave
upon wave sweeps over the bow.

Only one sculpted seraph peers upward,
as if she still remembers

the crooked golden ladder dangling
from the edge of sky. "Follow me,"
she seems to say, reaching

past sisters who stare, enamored,
at chiseled hips and shoulders.

This new heaven seemed so lovely.
But who can help them now? Graceful arms
amputated, cheeks stained with weeping.

In the dream he's a blacksmith

and she is a child, cradling
an old horseshoe no one will miss.

A small black pony stamps its feet.
Smoke sways on the ceiling.

Come closer, he says.
See the girl in the fire?

See how blue and white flames
fringe her mouth?

The pony snickers S-O-S.
Shall I put you in the fire, too?

He swings her onto his table,
beats the red glow thinner.

Every thief must be tamed or broken.
Two cold nails in her hand.

THE NIECE FINDS HER VOICE

Driving to Winnipesaukee

Who's watching you? the owl asks
from somewhere high above.

No streetlamps. No winking stars.
The horizon a closed eye mile after mile.

You, you the bird insists
can't deny what happened.

A yellow streak—no head, no tail—
hit my car's front tire.

Did I look down? Or fall asleep
so close to my aunt's favorite lake?

My flashlight casts a useless halo,
the only light between two dark pages.

*You, you did not want to see
the life rushing past you.*

No footprints, blood, tufts of fur.
Nothing I can name or dread.

Then something rustles the underbrush.
Four legs. Two. A woman?

I cannot move, trapped between
belief, denial. *I did not visit*

near the end. Pines stand mute.
Maples point knotted fingers.

*Stop dreaming. Move ahead.
You know what you have done.*

Secret

I should have told her: *I escaped.*
Two a.m., he was beating my door.

I woke to see two gauzy figures.
There was no moon that night.

The banging rose. *I'll rip you apart.*
The safety chain and I groaned.

Help me . . . I . . . cannot . . . breathe . . .
My words tangled like the sheets.

I never told her, or anyone:
One figure stayed at the foot

of the bed, the other by my side.
My phone in the other room.

I should have told her, *I escaped.*
You can too. Don't continue to hide.

One specter stood sentry at the door.
The other covered my eyes.

After one year

I sit by a trash can crowned
with maggots. Nice gift,
this mortality.

A man weeps softly, listening
to music. It's salvation he wants,
not broken lyrics.

There's a fish in the swan pond,
twenty-two inches. Does he know
he swims the same useless circle?

❀   ❀   ❀

What is that man writing,
his back to the view? How foolish
to think words will save him.

So many old people watch
the lake, the sky. They spin like
the carousel horses behind them.

A boy with a hollow eye stares past me,
wanders the waves and fallen limbs.
Even this lake eroding.

❀   ❀   ❀

Now children gather hands in a circle,
dance till they're dizzy, losing breath.
They can't even tell they're falling.

I am one day closer to losing my body.
Every creature seems to be thrashing.

What if life had no ending, no middle,
and no point in time? Would this woman
stop rocking and clutching her head?

At the animal park, Route 13

Put your finger in her mouth.
  That always makes her smile.

Eight weeks old, coat thick as a lamb's.
She gnaws my thumb: dry, useless nipple.

Muscles coil as she pulls my wrist closer,
mews to her mother, aunts, guardians—
generations of wingless lamassu.

She doesn't know her power yet.
  Hold that pose, hold it.

Years ago, three others stood watch over a girl:
raped, bloody, beaten. I picture them now, circling
my aunt, standing between her and my uncle.

Females do most of the hunting, you know.
  What are you looking for?

The cub squirms and growls, hind legs practicing
grandmother steps—silent, tiny, stealthy.

Miles from my pride, I feel my thighs tighten,
as if I'm hunched by a water hole, waiting.

Want another photo? You may never
  cuddle a lion again.

Victim to victor, holder to held.
Give me this moment, whatever the cost,
where the predator shakes, hunted.

Strays

For months, I asked
her to return. Heard
only the cat who died
in my arms; his heart
and kidneys choking.

He still visits. Briefly
the brass headboard shakes,
I feel his weight
on the blanket.

✤　　✤　　✤

Tina, my troubled
student from the prison,
reappears as well,
crouching in the bushes.

How many nights
did I call her name,
wanting to unknot
the sheet around her neck.

She'd weep and swallow
those razorblades
again, her bloody lips
trembling, triumphant.

✤　　✤　　✤

She died the year
three feral kittens
were born outside
her cell, one with her
ginger-colored hair.

The guards walked right by,
didn't hear any crying.
But I got close, plucked
one, angry and spitting,
from all she had known.

Auntie would have liked that.

At dusk they arrive

wearing thin paper skins,
names inked on Japanese lanterns.

Jane, Betty, Sofia drift by.
We were taught never to argue.

Dozens huddle along the lake's shore.
Silence in front of the children.

I've come to find Elaine, I say.
Watch her cross to the other side.

One lamp glides across the surface,
stops halfway, then collapses.

Another clings to the shore,
bereft of wind or courage.

Please don't say you've seen us.
We tried but could not help her.

Elaine slowly flickers a kind
of Morse code. *I'm all right, let me go.*

A thousand eyes blink on the water.
We've all told that lie many times.

One fragile lamp leans toward the murk.
Help me speak, revise.

Visitations

I

A lamp's fine light in my hair,
on the table. I cannot raise my head.
Even here a numb hum.

Now I am ready for the sound
of milk on a white cat's tongue.
A woodchuck's long sleep,

thinning clouds, stones in a brook
are a single chorused note
until she speaks:

Where am I? Did I drown?
Why does that man keep
holding me down?

II

Two nights later she reappears.
Walking on ice, three feet thick.
I have come to find that numbing sting
that tethers me to this life.

She kneels by a fishing hole.
The water beyond reach.

Like my daughter's hand
when I went under, holding
only the sound of her heart—
a frayed, invisible rope.

III

I see circles everywhere, she says,
though I walk in straight lines.

Daffodils skirt an oak tree
eight rings thick, the hem
of an angel's robe.

Yards away, children toss
a ball painted like the earth.
It sails over one boy's head.

Another boy lifts the globe high
and smiles as she turns round
and round, trying to catch her shadow.

Revisiting Lowell Street

Two blocks from her yellow house
a cemetery swallows decades of secrets.
If any escape, the grass *hush-hushes*;
leaves on the trees beat like crow wings:
Don't think you can evade us.

We didn't hear their rustling as children.
Our bicycle pedals and tires whirring
past headstones, faster and faster,
chasing sunshine and freedom.

If we had slowed, we might have heard
warnings, faint as hummingbirds:
Don't let fear become your shadow.
Anger buries you alive.

Beyond the gate, I think I see him
wearing a wrinkled police uniform.
He waves and tips an eight-point hat,
like the man he should have been.

Didn't you die in prison, I ask.
Diagnosis dementia. Never apologized.
Owl slowly circles above, scolding:
You—keep writing her story.

Ex opere operato

I don't know how she found the courage,
kneeling inches from the front door,
her mother's outline—crimson, forsaken.

How many times did she scour the rug,
loosening years of abuse? Then a cup
of peroxide, poured, watching it fizz and foam.

I'm sorry you had to see me this way.
I just couldn't stay any longer.

How many times did she press down
a towel before her mother's face
appeared, faint as the Shroud of Turin?

I should have told you my story sooner.
There's so much you don't know.

Pour, bubble, fizz—an expulsive sting
sinking deeper into the fibers.

I edited my college newspaper.
Loved my job at the law firm.

Did my cousin lean back, startled,
when that clear profile emerged?

Press, pray, lift. Another wet towel
cradled like sacred swaddling clothes
or baptismal robes for the dead.

I typed contracts that set others free . . .
Tried and tried to save him.

A final towel, a muted guise.
I forgot my worth. Remember
yours. Do that in memory of me.

Flight

Owl knows the stair you leave
is the one that creaks.

Step off, step off.
Let your whole life speak.

Underwater

The challenge was easy then:
dive off the boat at high tide,
swim down, down till you touch
the white sand, then translate
the messages signaled from above.

I remember sitting on the bottom,
watching the greenish sun wobble
or trade one shape for another
until the sky became a watercolor map
only my cousin and I could decipher.

Each wave made the thin paint
shimmer, another wash of light
rippling across the canvas.
Nothing looked the way it should,
and sounds—like poorly aimed arrows—

deflected off the surface.
Yet when she leaned over the side
of the boat, arms waving like seaweed,
I knew what she meant. *Stay there.*
Go this way. I'm the queen.

We didn't need words, not when
an invisible chain ran from boat to sand,
a family secret that flowed through
our veins, an ancient script tattooed
on our fingers, long before we were born.

Soon enough my lungs would burn
and I'd kick toward the surface,
reclaiming the world of sound.

Salt never stung, as I recall,
until I broke through the swells.
The sky is mine. I own the sun.
Hold your breath, hold it.
We understood metaphor then.

Two owls in conversation

Like Minerva, she tried to love
them both, arguing in the trees.

This is my home, called the first.
I own these hills and fields.

The second defended stolen turf:
Your world belongs to me.

Birches, pines slowly bent,
seduction filling the dark:

She and I will soar all night.
No, she will hide with me.

The two debated like philosophers
still trapped in that old cave.

Shadows are my reality.
Mine is a cloudless sky.

One voice crept, the other soared,
each suitor *hoot-who-ing* his say.

When did she learn that one
must choose? How did she decide?

Vision at the Notch

Halfway up Franconia
my aunt is rushing down.
I reached the summit, she says
breathing hard, cheeks glistening.

Your climb is steep ahead.
Don't wander from the path.
A bear cub runs out from the bush.
Go before his mother comes.

"Your eyes will be opened . . ."

In the cider heap, Christ's body,
Eve's sin, the apple.
What I desire I cannot taste:
to be Mary, on a horse,
voice lifted to the trinity,
praising the bruise-free skin of angels.

Fruit trees filled with angels:
food for my mortal body,
communion with trinity.
I shine the ripest apple,
leave the core for a horse.
Flesh is what I taste.

I have a taste
for angels.
I see a child on a horse,
the limbs of her body
curl up into stem and apple,
one with the trinity.

In my hand, the smallest trinity:
peel, flesh, seed—taste
of a newly fallen apple,
food and drink of angels.
I eat the fruit's white body,
hear the whinny of a horse.

A pale woman on a white horse
is filled with the trinity:
the child within her, a body
feeding on the taste
of Eden, the sound of angels
among branches, seeds in the apple.

Stooping for an apple,
I see the shadow of a horse;
in his mane, angels.

Fruit, limb, tree: new trinity.
It is time to taste
the ripened body.

Her last words

I wasn't afraid as I rose above
       the room, my house, the tree line.
Two pairs of wings soared with me—
       a slow, velvet shimmer.

Going, going home, they sang.
            Wasn't I just there?

A field of feathers below
       bloomed gold, brown, white—
to catch me if I faltered.

Above, a trapdoor, tightly sealed.
       To enter you must leave it all.

Every sound scattered then,
       like prey evading a raptor.
I heard myself clearly say:

Time to rise above this life.
Sever all phantom pain.

About the Author

Elizabeth Lund is the award-winning host of *Poetic Lines*, which features in-depth interviews with established and emerging poets. She also covers poetry for major publications, including *The Christian Science Monitor*, where she edited poetry for ten years. From 2015 through 2019 she wrote a monthly poetry column for *The Washington Post*. Her own poems have appeared in the US, the UK, and Canada. She has read and appeared at a variety of festivals, most recently the Gaithersburg Book Festival, where she served as the final judge for the 2020 high school poetry contest.

www.ingramcontent.com/pod-product-compliance
Lightning Source LLC
Chambersburg PA
CBHW031934080426
42734CB00007B/686